Estate
Gardens
of California

Estate
Gardens
of California

Melba Levick   Karen Dardick

RIZZOLI
NEW YORK

First published in the United States of America in 2002 by
RIZZOLI INTERNATIONAL PUBLICATIONS, INC.
300 Park Avenue South, New York, NY 10010

ISBN: 0-8478-2449-7
LCCN: 2001095465

Front cover: *The Sunken Garden at Filoli, Woodside*
Back cover: *Villa Narcissa, Rancho Palos Verdes*
Pages 2–3: *Val Verde, Montecito*
Pages 6–7: *Villa Narcissa, Rancho Palos Verdes*

Designed by Judy Geib

Distributed by St. Martin's Press

Printed and bound in Singapore

To Bret, Shaunti, and Bowie
ML

To Paramahansa Yogananda, Sri Durga Mata,
and Bob Mason
KD

Acknowledgments

We thank the owners and curators of the estates who gra-
ciously consented to share the beauty of their gardens with us
and with the readers of this book. In particular, our thanks go
to: Hal and Geraldine Alden; Finis and Julie Conner; Robert
and Beverly Cohen; Albert Collins; Jerry and Helen Stathatos;
Elin Vanderlip; Dagmar Sullivan and her daughter Paula
Escher; Helen Stauber, designer for the Alden estate; Pamela
Seager, director of Rancho Los Alamitos; Dr. Steven Timbrook,
director of Lotusland Foundation; Jim Fulsom and Catherine
Babcock, at The Huntington Botanical Gardens; Tom Rogers at
Filoli; Tim Lindsey, director of Virginia Robinson Gardens;
Don and Rhonda Carano, owners, and Nancy Gilbert, director
of public relations, at Villa Fiori, Ferrari-Carano; Gail and
Eduard Jenson, at Val Verde.

We also wish to express our sincere gratitude to our agent,
Sarah Jane Freymann, our editors at Rizzoli, David Morton
and Douglas Curran, and our designer, Judy Geib, for their
hard work and expertise.

Contents

Estate Gardens of California

The word "estate" conjures up images of vast expanses of tree-studded land surrounding an immense residence. An impressive and private driveway leads through a landscape with swaths of emerald green lawns that foreground a grand mansion, often accented by lavish garden rooms and beds of colorful plants. Stone walls might surround the estate, protecting the owners from danger and unwanted visitors. This is the type of estate common in Europe. On the east coast of the United States, American leaders of business and industry also created their versions of Old World aristocratic residences.

But it's different in California. Here, in the world's fifth largest economy, people with great wealth have indeed built great estates, but many are adaptations unique to California, reflecting its Mexican and Spanish Mediterranean heritage.

Franciscan missionaries marched into what was called Alta California in the 1700s seeking religious converts. The land belonged to Spain, and then Mexico, until the United States acquired the rich and relatively sparsely populated region. Throughout the 1800s traders, trappers, explorers, ranchers, gold miners, and captains of industry swelled the state's tiny population. The advent of the motion picture industry in the early 1900s ignited people's imagination and interest in this newly emerging paradise, and World War II changed its face forever, when millions of people swarmed to California—the land where dreams could be realized.

These dreams included the good life: home ownership, a garden, and a way of living compatible with a land of abundant sunshine. Along with people seeking to make fortunes came people *with* great fortunes. They reveled in the delights of plucking fruit from home orchards and decorating their gardens with December roses while much of the nation shivered in snow.

For the Golden State is also a garden state. As newcomers quickly discovered, this vast sun-drenched land is blessed with fertile soil, so it was not an accident that California became one of the leading agricultural regions of America, including Wasco, where close to 90 percent of all our garden roses are grown.

HISTORY OF CALIFORNIA GARDENING

Gardening in California really begins with the advent of the Franciscan missionaries in the mid-1700s. They founded missions along, and within the protection of, mission walls, and created gardens with seeds brought from Mexico. These were functional gardens. Important plants included olive trees for oil, grape vines for sacramental wine, citrus, figs, dates, pomegranates, strawberries, raspberries, and other fruit for their refectory tables. There were also herbs, such as lavender for medicinal use, and flowers to decorate the altars. Old records show plantings of antique Rose of Castile, Belle of Portugal, lilies, hollyhocks, marigolds, jonquils, and other beautiful flowers that flourished in Spain. The padres also got plants from

The fountain at Beaulieu.

Vibrantly colored bearded irises thrive at Filoli.

explorers who had brought them from their homelands. Early California settlers traded with the friars and thus were able to create their own gardens from an ever-growing palette that included pepper trees, calla lilies, oleander shrubs, and jasmine vines.

After the missions were secularized by the Mexican government, about 200 years ago, the *rancho* period of California gardening history began, when vast miles of oak-studded, chaparral-covered soil came into the hands of a fortunate few. Two hundred *ranchos*, with wealth from cattle and crops, covered the state. And although their acreage was measured in the thousands, the residences were relatively modest, such as at Rancho Los Alamitos (pp. 78–89). Home orchards and gardens provided food and medicine for family and workers, and ornamental gardens scarcely existed.

For California's great gardens to emerge, it took the railroad's increased ease of transportation, improved irrigation systems, and the arrival of wealthy East Coast gentry. And as they flocked to regions around San Francisco, Santa Barbara, and Los Angeles, great houses and landscapes sprang into being. Some newcomers created gardens evoking their eastern heritage. Others borrowed heavily from European traditions, especially from the Mediterranean, with its similar arid, sun-drenched climate.

Throughout the Mediterranean, the Islamic influence that had been adopted in Spain during centuries of Moorish rule had spread. In that tradition, a garden was a place of enclosure, a walled oasis that provided shade from the desert heat, that contained life-giving water in the form of fountains and pools, and offered fragrant and colorful flowers to entice the senses.

In time, however, the concept of garden evolved into that of a retreat from hostile nature or warring invaders. Enclosure, whether by monastery walls or fortified cas-

tles, continued over the centuries as gardens evolved from pleasure to more utilitarian purposes. They were the source of herbs, medicines, and of course food. The idea of the pleasure garden, ornate with flowers and used for leisure and entertainment, is a relatively modern notion. It was this expression that flourished in California, especially in the warmer southern parts of the state.

PLANT PALETTE

It is the plant palette of almost endless possibilities that makes California gardens different from those in other parts of America. Few other places in the world have such a wealth of plant life, which is mainly due to the fabled, mild climate with its classic, dry subtropical summers. Technically termed "Mediterranean," only three percent of the world has this climate, the Mediterranean itself, South Africa, California, and especially Australia. Plants from rainier climates have deep green leaves with broad shapes. Plants from drier regions have foliage colors that range from soft shades of steel blue to gray and olive, and brilliant flower colors like orange and red. Although there are some plants that prefer one region to another—ocean-front rather than mountains, rain soaked redwood forests, or sandy deserts—overall, there are very few plants that can't be grown in California. The combinations and design choices are astounding.

Many plants that now seem synonymous with California actually were imported over the centuries. While the missionaries brought grapes, citrus, roses and more, early traders introduced novelties like dragon trees from the Canary Islands and bird of paradise from South Africa. The great explosion occurred, however, in the mid-1800s when nurserymen learned that they could grow a wide range of exotic plants outdoors, while in the East they had to be under glass, which was cumbersome and costly. The race was on among nursery owners in San

Francisco and Sacramento, the more populous regions of the state in the mid-1800s, to import plants from Australia, Europe, and the East Coast. Flowering trees, many varieties of roses, and flowering shrubs soon adorned numerous gardens. After the 1870s, palm trees became specimen trees of choice for both ornamental and practical purposes. Communities were still far-flung, and ranches and estates often relied on the tall silhouette of a specimen palm to serve as a beacon to visitors. Although palm trees are now the symbol of Southern California, almost all were imported from other parts of the world. Only one species is native to California, and it grows in a canyon near Palm Springs.

CALIFORNIA GARDEN DESIGN

In California garden designers have great creative expression with its amazingly rich plant resources, and have used them in novel combinations and juxtapositions. It's possible to plant an aloe with an alstroemeria, to scatter fleshly-leafed succulents like hen 'n chick with bedding plants like pansies or violas. On the whole, classic estate gardens follow more traditional design principles of long vistas, parterres, rectangular paths leading to a central fountain, and manicured trees and shrubs as borders or screens. Certainly Villa Narcissa (pp. 16–23) exemplifies the finest of classic Mediterranean garden design. Here, too, are magnificent views that are included as borrowed vistas and are an important design aspect—whether it's the Newport Bay vista at the Cohen estate (pp. 38–47) or the dense forest near Villa Fiore (pp. 68–77) in Sonoma County's wine region. Val Verde (pp. 58–67), the epitome of classic design in California, exists in large part to capitalize on the man-made forest and distant ocean views afforded by the hilltop setting in Montecito.

However, in many regions, the major focus of estate gardens is an expanse of lawn used to open up distant vistas by careful placement of specimen trees, as can be seen at Lotusland (pp. 118–31). But California designs can also be bold and audacious, as the rest of Lotusland exemplifies, due to the creativity of Madame Ganna Walska, who transformed a traditional estate garden into her unusual spiritual retreat. A renowned blue garden is planted only with foliage plants in hues of bluish green, the startling sculptured forms of immense cacti line the main driveway, and an unusual collection of aloes adorn a garden room dedicated to this collection.

Other great California estate gardens were created by owners who were also passionate plant collectors. Henry Huntington gradually converted his ranch (pp. 160–73) into a botanical garden to house his enormous collection of cacti and succulents, palm trees and flowering trees imported from Australia and New Zealand. Another businessman and plant enthusiast, E. Manchester Boddy, who originated the estate now known as Descanso Gardens (pp. 90–101), spread the popularity of camellias throughout the state. He imported *C. Reticulata* from China in the

Detail of parterre and reflecting pool at Val Verde, Montecito.

1940s, which influenced the subsequent breeding of many new camellia cultivars.

William Randolph Hearst exerted great influence, albeit indirectly, on California gardens. His desire to "build a little something on the hilltop" resulted in one of the most magnificent estates in America, which is now called Hearst Castle at San Simeon. He hired Julia Morgan to create his dream, an estate of 165 rooms and 127 acres of gardens, terraces, pools and walkways. Hearst wanted a garden design in harmony with his magnificent Mediterranean revival style buildings. He wanted a garden inspired by the Italian and Spanish ones he had visited or read about, which offered a profusion of blooms throughout the year. He spent a small fortune to accomplish this. During the 1910s and 1920s, his agents scoured the nurseries for exotic plants including New Zealand tea trees, white heliotrope, cannas, and brugmansia. His gardens had a rich profusion of trees and shrubs, along with colorful bougainvillea, tulips, hyacinths, gladioluses, lilies, dahlias, asters, geraniums, lantana, petunias, sweet peas, tuberous begonias, and gloxinias. The house was a marvel during his lifetime and after his death, when San Simeon was given to the State of California and opened for public tours in 1958.

OUTDOOR LIVING

California gardens are characterized as outdoor living rooms, extensions of homes, whether grand or small. People like Florence Bixby insisted that her gardens at Rancho Los Alamitos (pp. 78–89) should be comfortable places where people could relax rather than just gaze. When Virginia Robinson created her Beverly Hills gardens (pp. 132–43), she, too, developed them with the idea of using them as outdoor entertainment areas. Her parties were acclaimed and invitations were eagerly sought.

During the 1920s and 1930s estates proliferated, especially in Southern California, as the growing entertainment industry made Beverly Hills and parts of surrounding Los Angeles choice locations for the rich and famous. While gardens continued to have water features, like tile-lined fountains, the swimming pool now sprang into popular use. Lush landscaping suggested tropical paradises. The multi-use of space also led to a merging of design styles that borrowed from tropical as well as Mediterranean regions. This eclectic design, so very much a part of the California landscape, also became true of the architecture, but the garden and the house design were not always precisely complementary.

Another departure from tradition is the size of California estates. As real estate prices have soared, especially in Beverly Hills and Los Angeles, many owners have been tempted to subdivide their land. A grand house on only one acre with a garden can sell for several millions of dollars, and is considered an estate. Such smaller grounds have encouraged owners to plant densely, especially if one is a true garden enthusiast.

In these pages, you will see an array of estate gardens. Historic Rancho Los Alamitos exemplifies the Mexican heritage adapted to twentieth-century tastes. The Huntington is one of the world's great botanical gardens, and is also most influential in California as design inspiration and as a source of unusual plants for garden hobbyists throughout the state. In addition to the great estates, though, you can also be inspired by such smaller properties as the Cohen and Stathatos (pp. 38–47; 102–109) estates, which have been beautifully landscaped by their owners, who are true "plants people." This book, then, is about beauty transcending property boundaries, about beauty that can be replicated on the smaller scale, and beauty that can inspire appreciation for the art form of the garden.

Villa Narcissa

Rancho Palos Verdes

A grand garden in the classic Italian tradition, Villa Narcissa has earned a reputation as the most celebrated Mediterranean garden in Southern California. A mature landscape by California standards, it's renowned for stately allées of cypress, olive, and citrus trees and exquisite garden art and ornamentation.

The formality of line, design, and plant palette is accented by enormous terra cotta urns and pots imported from Tuscany, along with seventeen statues placed in strategic vistas. Art is an important part of this garden, in keeping with the passion of owner Elin Vanderlip, who founded Friends of French Art to fund restoration of French art. A woman of culture and keen artistic taste, she's also been a proponent of restoration of art, artifacts, and in this case, a great garden.

In 1946, she moved into Villa Narcissa as the bride of Kelvin Cox Vanderlip. While raising a family of four children, traveling extensively throughout the world, and participating in numerous social and charitable functions, Mrs. Vanderlip expanded the original landscape by adding additional garden rooms, sculpture, and garden ornaments over a period of several decades.

Frederick Law Olmstead, Jr. (son of the designer of New York's Central Park) planned the initial landscape. The firm Olmstead Brothers of Boston was retained by wealthy New York banker Frank A. Vanderlip (Kelvin's father) after he bought the original 16,200-acre land grant of Palos Verdes Estates in 1912. In the 1920s, he and the Olsmsteads

*A cypress allée flanks 250 steps leading to a temple of
Doric columns where theatrical performances are held.
The trees were imported from Rome in 1920.*

created the city of Rancho Palos Verdes, and also selected the site for his future estate, Villa Narcissa, named after his wife. But though the grounds were laid out and guest-houses built, the grand mansion was only a dream with the advent of the Depression. The twelve-acre site remained in the family, and it was here that the young Elin Vanderlip established her home.

Although widowed in 1956, she remained dedicated to enhancement of both house and garden. Over the years, the Italian villa has been enlarged and remodeled. An ardent gardener and lover of the arts through the influence of her Norwegian grandmother, Mrs. Vanderlip was influenced by her grandmother's gardens. The gardens at Villa Narcissa also reflect many ideas Mrs. Vanderlip obtained while touring numerous great public and private gardens throughout Italy and France.

Like many Mediterranean grand gardens, Villa Narcissa is constructed on a formal axis, with linear views leading the eye beyond the immediate gardens into the surrounding vistas. The gardens are filled with hundreds of mature stone pine, Aleppo pine, olive, and cypress trees. The north vista extends up a sloping hill of 300 feet, where a great cypress allée, bordering more than 250 steps, leads to a Doric temple near a Greek amphitheater used for outdoor performances and entertainment.

Red ocher walls and mustard yellow trim on Villa Narcissa
were inspired by the folk art of owner Elin Vanderlip's
native Norway.

*Previous pages: The twelve-acre estate offers superb views
of the Pacific Ocean near Portuguese Bend in Los Angeles
County. Drifts of purple statice highlight the foreground.*

*Villa Narcissa is a harmonious blend of the wild and the culti-
vated, punctuated by classic art and ornamentation, like these
Corinthian columns situated at intervals up the 300-foot hillside.*

Radiating along the hillside are several allées of olive trees, citrus, and jacaranda trees. A garden vignette consisting of banana and Brazilian pepper trees, purple statice, and vivid pink geraniums is named Temple of Eliana, in honor of a granddaughter.

Among the reasons for which Frank Vanderlip had selected the site of the estate are the impressive views it offers of the Pacific Ocean. On the south side of the house, a brick terrace more than 200-feet-long frames the sea and a view of Catalina Island. The terrace is patterned after a similar terrace Mrs. Vanderlip admired at the Villa Aldobrandini in Frascati.

Although Mrs. Vanderlip prefers gardens in shades of green for their richness and simplicity, she also loves bold, bright colors. Bright pink geraniums, deep-blue hibiscus, and brilliant bougainvillea in enormous terra cotta pots or interplanted beneath sheltering trees or within clipped box hedges are vivid floral accents.

"My basic rule for garden design is simplicity, simplicity, simplicity," she says with a laugh. "I abhor busy gardens crammed with flowers. They should be used as accents only."

An example of this is the marvelous brick terrace edged by silver-green foliage of olive trees that shimmer in the afternoon sunlight. Matching rows of potted hydrangeas are wonderfully sophisticated accents.

Extensive use of paved surfaces rather than green swaths of water-thirsty lawns characterize Mediterranean gardens. Villa Narcissa landscaping includes acres of brick pathways, terraces, and patios that serve as inviting seating areas or to transport guests from one garden room to another.

The gardens are also a harmonious blending of the wild and the cultivated. Surrounding the estate are chaparral-covered hills that slope down to the vivid blue Pacific Ocean. Transitional areas link the natural and the planted and one has the sense that this garden is somehow timeless and belongs in this space. Here the heart of the garden merges with the spirit of nature in a glorious blend of light, movement, and exuberance.

Filoli

Woodside

Filoli has one of America's greatest gardens. Strolling along its allée lined with 200 meticulously manicured yew trees is like stepping back in time, to an era of grand estates and lavish garden parties, where one can imagine wonderful family celebrations in the formal gardens on this 654-acre estate. Set amongst this splendor, the Georgian-Revival mansion looks as if it could be more at home in Europe than just 30 miles from San Francisco. And for good reason. Filoli was built by William Bowers Bourn II who, in his youth, had studied at Cambridge University and became an ardent fan of the architecture and style of life in Great Britain. He emulated this by building on the San Francisco Peninsula on a gentle rise where he loved the view of the surrounding hillside and Crystal Springs Lake—a view that reminded him of Ireland, where he owned Muckross estate.

Bourn, president of the Spring Valley Water Company and owner of the Empire Mine, one of the richest gold mines in America, in 1915 selected famed San Francisco architect Willis Polk to create his 43-room, 36,000-square-foot mansion, which was completed in 1917. The sixteen-acre formal gardens were an important element in the overall scheme. They are defined by more than a dozen distinct garden "rooms"of brick walls, gates, and hedges that were designed by Bruce Porter to blend harmoniously with the striking natural setting of surrounding woodlands, agricultural fields, and orchards. Noted plant expert Isabella Worn supervised

Pots of foxgloves accent the Sunken Garden's in summer.

Following pages: Filoli's Sunken Garden.

Climbing roses frame the iron gate leading to the Cathedral Garden.

The 36,000-square-foot modified Georgian mansion contains 43 rooms.

the selection and placement of the trees, shrubs and plants from its inception and throughout its evolution over several decades.

Bourn named his estate Filoli as an acronym for his life's motto: "**Fi**ght for a just cause; **Lo**ve your fellow man; **Li**ve a good life." He and his wife enjoyed their magnificent estate until their deaths in 1936. In 1937, Mr. and Mrs. William P. Roth bought Filoli. Mrs. Roth was an avid gardener who added her own personal touch to its existing beauty. She enhanced what the Bourns had created, and in 1975, donated Filoli to the

National Trust for Historic Preservation so the public can experience its splendor.

Both mansion and gardens are open to the public on self-guided tours from mid-February through October. There is always something lovely to look at, but even if there weren't flowers in profusion, it's worth a trip to study the garden design itself—the so-called bones of a garden.

At a time when gardens were distinctly different regions from a house or estate, the gardens and house at Filoli were designed as complementary units. The north-south axis of the overall garden echoes the line of

Previous pages: The Knot Gardens are designed in the style of
traditional English knot gardens with intricate, interlocking patterns.

These two traditional-style English Knot Gardens were planted at Filoli by the Woodside-Atherton Garden Club in 1976.

Clipped hedges are major design elements in the sixteen-acres of gardens. Spring and summer annual flowers spill over borders and beds.

the mansion's Transverse Hall. Each room provides garden vistas. The garden is a succession of outdoor rooms, with parterres, terraces, lawns, and pools, arranged between the two parallel north-south walks. The West Terrace contains more than 200 Irish yew trees, grown from cuttings taken at Muckross, and is probably Filoli's most famous feature.

Strolling from the terraces that flank the mansion, visitors can enjoy the Sunken Garden, considered the most impressive of Filoli's garden rooms with its shallow reflecting pool mirroring the clock tower. Evoking an Italian Renaissance flower garden, it has simple geometric flower beds, edged with boxwood, that are planted each spring and fall with thousands of spring bulbs and annuals.

Nearby, the Walled Garden offers the Dutch Garden, Sundial Garden, Wedding Place and Chartres Cathedral Garden where standard roses, colorful annuals and boxwood borders evoke a stained glass window. Visitors can also amble through the Woodland Garden, Cutting Garden which still provides flowers for arrangements within the mansion, Rose Garden containing 500 modern varieties, and Knot Garden designed in the traditional style of English knot gardens with intricate, interlocking patterns. The over-and-under design effect is detailed with herbs and other plants. In spring, Daffodil Meadow is a blaze of golden glory. In fall, copper beeches, gingko and Japanese maple trees contribute

brilliant blazes of yellow, red or orange leafed splendor to the landscape.

Gardening enthusiasts will appreciate viewing Filoli's rare plant specimens such as a climbing hydrangea trained on the brick wall separating the pool area from the Woodland Garden where rare pollarded London Plane Trees can also be found.

Inside, the mansion contains fine furnishings, artwork, decorative pieces and elaborate floral arrangements and can be viewed on shelf-guided tours. Filoli is a living testament to gracious living, glorious gardens and an elegant lifestyle.

Filoli is located at Cañada Road, Woodside, California 94062. The estate is open for viewing February through October. There is an admission fee. For information, call (650) 364-8300 or visit the web site: www.filoli.org.

Cohen Estate

Newport Beach

Some estate gardens feature broad expanses of emerald green lawns. Others include dense woodlands. But Robert and Beverly Cohen's one-acre-plus estate, in one of California's most exclusive residential areas, is unique: it slopes directly onto Newport Bay.

"There isn't a prettier waterfront lot on the entire Pacific Coast," Robert Cohen says. He knows because he searched the region to find a place with waterfront access large enough for the family's yacht, which is what inspired them to purchase this 9,000 square-foot house in 1990.

This estate is famous in the region because it was once the home of John Wayne, who lived there with his wife Pilar, from 1953 to 1986.

The house was built in 1950. The eclectic architecture evokes France, with its sloping Mansard roof, yet it's more contemporary in overall appearance because it features wide expanses of glass windows and French doors that capitalize on the stunning, panoramic views of Newport Harbor.

When the Cohens bought the estate, they completely renovated the landscape and added a 15,000-square-foot lath house. RC, as Robert prefers to be called, collects succulent plants and estimates his collection to be in excess of one million. His spectacular "succulent paradise," as he calls it, showcases all sorts of succulent plants, including rotund agaves, colorful kalanchoes, pendent string-of-pearls, clumping

Garlands of donkey tails and echeveria are some of the many succulent plants used by owner Robert Cohen in his Newport Beach landscape.

Following pages: The slope adjacent to Newport Bay contains pots filled mainly with white flowers—Iceberg roses, alyssum, and geraniums—plus ubiquitous succulents.

A 55-year-old ficus tree supports several immense staghorn ferns.

echeverias, crassula, dudleya, aeoniums, and many, many more. They function as graceful groundcovers cascading down mixed borders, stately elongated sentinels that mark walkways and pathways, and visual exclamation points scattered among Iceberg roses and verdant lawns. A multitude of pots of all sizes are clustered on the large patio and terraces.

Succulents are native to desert and semi-desert regions and collectors and landscape designers appreciate them for their sculptural appearance and usefulness in drought-tolerant landscapes. RC admires his plants for their appearances, but can't be bothered with cataloging them, and rarely remembers specific varieties. He's enthusiastic about how a plant looks in its space, especially in combination with foliage, annual or perennial flowering plants. They bring a unique appearance to his home as well as to the Four Seasons Hotel in Los Angeles, of which he is the managing general partner and co-owner.

He and his wife Beverly love to entertain, and often have parties at the hotel or at their home, where the gardens are important part of the décor, and where the tables are often decorated with brilliantly colored coleus, accented with trailing strings of donkey tails or fleshly-leafed hen 'n chicks.

The gardens, although a fascinating blend of textures, plant forms, and brightly colored foliage plants, also contain more mundane plants like begonias, and

Fascinated by their sculptural shapes and colors, RC Cohen raises thousands of different succulent plants—such as those shown here—and displays them throughout his estate.

geraniums. Numerous types of ferns, including staghorn ferns, also fill shady spots or are mounted at eye level. A 55-year-old ficus tree supports several immense staghorn ferns and orchids that bloom once or twice a year. Some of the palm trees are also more than 50 years old. Their thick trunks are clad in living garlands of brilliant bougainvillea and vigorous climbing roses. RC believes in combining plants with different leaf forms, structures and hues, like lobellia, calla lilies, hydrangeas and perennials. The ocean side landscape consists of succulents intermingled with mainly white flowers, including Iceberg roses, stock, and alyssum. The interior courtyard and front drive landscaped beds are planted in shades of pink, red, lavender, and blue, and of course include starkly sculptural succulent plants as dramatic accents. Always stunning, these gardens are especially appealing during the winter holidays when RC mixes in vivid red poinsettias.

The gardens are meticulous because RC is a hands-on gardener who loves to spend Saturdays in the middle of the garden beds, pruning, deadheading, and watering. When he's not able to tend his plants, he closely supervises the gardening staff to ensure the gardens are always in pristine condition. His other favorite pastime is potting and dividing the thousands of plants growing in his two lathe houses, which are connected by an aviary containing fantail and curly back pigeons, his latest fascination.

He's a dedicated gardener who loves flowers and all sorts of plants, which is not surprising from a man who had a thriving career in the retail floral industry before switching to real estate development.

RC ventured into real estate investments beginning in the 1960s. In 1978, he acquired land adjacent to Beverly Hills and spent the next nine years developing and completing the Four Seasons Hotel. Among other activities, he supervised the design and installation of its lush and elaborate landscape. Recently, he installed a lavish garden surrounding the hotel's new spa center. It features citrus trees in containers, underplanted with alyssum, coleus and, of course, succulents. The hotel's gardens are open for public viewing. It is quite pleasant to enjoy lunch or dinner in the Garden Room restaurant, followed by a leisurely stroll around the grounds.

Collins Estate

Beverly Hills

Most gardens are made for the pleasure of their owners, but not the one at the Collins estate, where neighbors and passers-by enjoy this lovely California version of an English garden. Owner Albert Collins delights in adorning his sloping front lawn with colorful decorations for Easter, Independence Day, Halloween, and Christmas. Four-foot pastel painted wooden tulips surrounded by white wooden bunnies would be just one of the appealing flourishes he regards as gifts of goodwill to the neighborhood and wayfarers.

The Collinses' stone-clad Tudor manor was built in 1952 and occupies 7000 square feet of its 1.6 acre site on Sunset Boulevard. And although that "Millionaire's Row" winds all the way through Beverly Hills, many of the gardens the public can see are just average yards with palm trees and flowering shrubs like agapanthus, which is ubiquitous throughout Southern California. The Collins estate, however, has remarkably charming gardens, both in the front and in the rear, where private gardens surround a swimming pool and guesthouse. Since they bought the property in 1981, Collins and his wife, Jeanne, have spent considerable time and effort renovating the gardens, which, although young by European standards, have a fullness and maturity because of careful design, good gardening practices, and the abundance of plant materials. The gardens reflect a passion both for the impressive plant collections and for colorful display. For example, each spring Collins plants masses of sweet-

Here, in the back garden of the Collins estate, masses of fragrant sweet peas grow to ten-foot heights on specially constructed trellises.

The English-design influence is reflected in the stylistic pockets of colorful garden beds filled with vivid Iceland poppies and dramatic ranunculus.

Pots of cacti and succulents line the swimming pool in the distance.

Sculptural drama is provided by massive hanging baskets of ferns, detailed with cascades of donkey tails.

smelling sweet peas that grow ten feet tall on specially constructed trellises in the rear and front gardens.

Collins's life-long involvement with flowers goes back to his high school years, when he sold sweet peas on a street corner in Los Angeles. Eventually, he saved enough money to buy a flower shop, but his career soared later when he invested in real estate and development in Los Angeles. Buildings then replaced flowers in his professional life, but Collins never lost his interest in things floral.

The English influence is reflected in the stylistic pockets of colorful garden beds filled each spring with vivid orange and yellow Iceland poppies, red, white and pink ranunculus, and dramatic blue delphiniums. These are replaced in summer with sunshine-yellow marigolds, blue lobelia, and white honey-scented alyssum. In fall,

Undulating paths lead through colorful beds of azaleas, cineraria, Iceland poppies, and other vibrantly colored annual flowering plants. Clumps of tall white calla lilies in the foreground provide foliage contrast.

cheerful pansies in a variety of colors vie for attention among violas. Throughout the year, roses anchor the landscape with form, color, and fragrance: trees of them line the driveway, more grace the rear gardens, and the gleaming white Iceberg variety accents the front vista.

Over the entire site, stately trees, including several sycamores more than a century old, provide structure and definition to the landscape. Liquid amber, ficus, and a variety of fruit trees, including California's famed orange and lemon trees, have also been brought in over the years. Several specimen kumquats line densely planted flowerbeds around the pool and entertainment area. Tangerine, peach, and apple trees tucked in near an arbor walk are harvested for the table. And staghorn ferns hang from the sycamore trees.

All of these plantings contribute to the eclectic nature of this garden, and they are aided by Collins's collection of more than a thousand succulents and cacti throughout the landscape. A cactus collection is clustered in an area adjacent to the pool. Succulents in a variety of forms and shapes are interspersed with flowering plants, breaking the traditional rules of landscape design. A massive lathe house, stretching along the west side of the lawn, is filled with these beguiling living sculptures in various hues of greens.

From every direction, whether inside the house looking out or on the street looking toward the house, one delights in a multitude of colors, shades, shapes, and designs in this landscape that is clearly by and for garden aficionados.

Val Verde

Montecito

Situated on seventeen acres of wooded grounds in
Montecito, just south of Santa Barbara, Val Verde is one
of the most photogenic and influential estate gardens in
California. The Spanish Colonial house on the site was
considered the first modern house on the West Coast
when it was initially built in 1919, and the landscape surrounding it has had a strong influence on subsequent
California gardens. Val Verde is a historic site and the
estate is listed on the National Register of Historic Places.

Val Verde's origins lie in Henry Dater's acquisition of
twenty-five acres of wooded hillside and the subsequent
commissioning of Bertram Goodhue to build what Dater
called *Dias Felices*, his family's winter retreat. But
before the estate, came the forest.

Charles Gibbs Adams laid out the gardens and
planted trees in 1896 so that when the owners moved in
the estate would be surrounded by mature trees, shrubs,
and other plantings. The site once contained an olive
orchard, and remnants of this still remain. But the woodland is primarily composed of dramatically contoured
California oak trees. Within the woodland, a network of
formal paths leads through a tropical planting of palms,
avocados, bananas, rubber trees, and other numerous
exotic specimens acquired by Dater, who was fascinated
by exotic plants.

In 1925, C. H. Luddington bought the estate and commissioned renowned landscape designer Lockwood de
Forest to convert the site to a permanent residence,

*The great reflecting pool below a 300-foot parterre is the
most famous feature at Val Verde.*

Following pages: Here, ivy geraniums cascade over the parterre.

which was renamed *Val Verde*. Although formal gardens surrounded the mansion, Luddington found something in them disturbing, a haphazard aspect that recalled an avid plant collector, if not a disciplined gardener—De Forest was called in to remedy this. The result of this commission was De Forest's California rendition of an Italianate-Mediterranean garden. An illustration of this can be seen in what is perhaps Val Verde's most noted aspect: a 300-foot-long terrace with a series of stairs and parterres descending to a formal reflecting pool, into which a fountain spills.

De Forest also incorporated elements of Persian and Mexican design in this landscape. Entrances to the house are defined. Visitors with commercial purposes enter from the doorway flanking the driveway. The original Grand Entrance, facing the ponds and water terrace, was used by the original owner and his guests; but De Forest changed the owner's entrance to the back, facing the great reflecting pool and the long view of the surrounding woodland. In Islamic tradition, this type of access is referred to as the Paradise Side. Throughout, demarcations between architecture and landscape are blurred. Plants are used as architectural features and vice versa. An example is a massive tree limb accented by a false wall that was created for the sole purpose of highlighting the limb, much as one would place a statue in a garden for embellishment.

The seventeen-acre estate is studded with centuries-old California live oak trees, which have been incorporated into the design, as shown here adjacent to the 300-foot parterre.

De Forest is also noted for design elements that accentuate the surrounding vista, a term referred to as a "borrowed landscape." He sited columns, walks, and statues to lead the viewer's eye over the surrounding woods and to the distant Pacific Ocean. He regarded a landscape as a three-dimensional painting, an idea that was a startling innovation century ago. From the dining room, situated on the north side of the house, a narrow pool flanked by olives leads the eye to a wall, where a decorative statue is displayed. On the house's south side, another, wider pool is flanked by narrow parterre beds with short boxwood hedges and dwarf citrus trees. Annual flowers add splashes of color to the formal setting. Statuary and great urns are placed in strategic sites throughout the formal gardens, serving

Above: Here, clivia line a pathway leading to a secluded fountain.

Right: Stairs lead to the great reflecting pool.

as visual focal points and evoking an atmosphere of centuries long gone by.

In 1955, Val Verde again changed hands and was purchased by Warren Austin—who lived on the site, with his family, until his death in 1999. Val Verde is still privately owned, though the recently established Warren R. Austin and Heath Horton Austin Val Verde Foundation which has been formed and is in the process of arranging for limited public viewing of these remarkable grounds. There are also plans to preserve the gardens to keep their appearance as they existed during the 1940s to 1960s, with special care for the century-old olive grove and the numerous blue agaves.

For current touring information, call (805) 969-9852.

Villa Fiore

Ferrari-Carano Vineyards & Winery in Sonoma County

Although the setting is Dry Creek Valley in California's fertile Sonoma County, Villa Fiore evokes the beauty, atmosphere, and ambiance of a Tuscan villa. Modern gardens of this beauty and magnitude are rare in California. A young garden by horticultural standards, the five-acre landscape has the lushness, maturity, and complexity of a garden that's decades old. It is also the showcase for an award-winning winery.

When Don and Rhonda Carano founded their winery, Ferrari-Carano in 1981, they gradually acquired 2,500 acres of some of Sonoma County's finest vineyards. Committed to a pursuit of excellence in creating wines, they carried out the same philosophy when they built their hospitality center, appropriately named Villa Fiore (House of Flowers). Resembling a Tuscan villa perched on a hillside, the 25,000-square-foot imposing edifice is surrounded by exquisite gardens blending the best of Mediterranean formality with the informality of adjacent California landscapes and the surrounding vineyards. Open to the public, these gardens are widely regarded as being among the finest in America in terms of design, complexity, and care.

Rhonda Carano, who has enjoyed gardening since she was a child, played a major role in the design of the gardens. She worked in partnership with LV Landscape Architects and head gardener Pat Patin.

"Because my grandmother and father were ardent gardeners, I grew up with a love of gardening," she com-

Here, clipped boxwood hedges surround beds of pansies. In the distance are fields of Malbec, Zinfandel, and Sauvignon Blanc grapes that thrive in the fertile soil of Dry Creek Valley.

These ornamental grasses provide foliage contrast to the bed of daylilies flanking the formal rose garden.

mented. "To this day, I view gardening as my personal time to create, to design, and to reflect. It always amazes me when people visit Ferrari-Carano that the gardens bring such joy to all. Young and old alike, the gardens light up the hearts of all and, for me, have become a source of pride."

Rhonda has good reason to be proud of the transformation of what had been a five-acre swath of lawns and fruit orchards into a stunning series of garden rooms and formal walks, filled with flowerbeds of dazzling seasonal color. Although the garden was formally inaugurated in 1997, it continues to be a work in progress. Like the Caranos' fine wines, these gardens have many layers of complexity, including great variation and subtlety of color, texture, composition, and balance and should be savored during the different seasons of the year.

Foundation plants, consisting of more than 800 shrubs and trees, combine Mediterranean and Asian palettes with plants suitable for Northern California. Planted densely and skillfully pruned, they offer contrasts in texture, form, and pattern.

Leaving behind the highway meandering through the vineyard-clad hillsides of Dry Creek, the visitor who enters the Ferrari-Carano winery in Healdsburg is transported into another world. The entrance flanking the parking area is deftly planted with a variety of palm trees, ornamental plum trees, and Coast Live Oak trees, underplanted with oakleaf and lacecap hydrangeas.

Daylilies send up spikes of color in harmony with massed plantings of perennials and annuals.

Blue spruce trees, rhododendrons, camellias, Japanese maples, tall slender birch trees, black pines, and hostas delineate the formal walk up the gently sloping hill to Villa Fiore. Columnar hornbeam trees define the entrance to the wine tasting room and gift shop.

Along the walkway, surrounded by more than one acre of vivid green lawn, beds of pansies flourish winter through spring. They're replaced with petunias, marigolds, and dahlias in summer. The captivating ornamental display continues from ground to sky as hanging baskets filled with cascading flowers vie for attention.

A 1.5 acre Enclosed Garden is one of the delights in this landscape. A four-foot privet hedge hides this garden filled with surprises, including two natural looking ponds created from local stones. Filled with water lilies and goldfish, they too are densely planted with shrubs, trees, and flowers, all suited for this semi-Mediterranean climate. A stream connects the ponds, and the sound of water cascading over the rocks blends harmoniously with the sounds of the birds flitting from tree to tree and flower to flower. A borrowed landscape of liquidambar, fir and camphor trees in the distance provides a majestic frame for the Enclosed Garden. Roses are among Rhonda's favorite flowers (including tulips and peonies), and a formal garden with perennial favorites like Mr.

This antique winepress was imported from Italy. A crane was required to lift it into place in its garden site at Villa Fiore.

Lincoln, Redgold, Peace, and Europeana, beckons visitors to a nearby gazebo.

Rhonda's passion for wine and art is matched by her passion for gardening. She concentrates on creating a tapestry landscape with layers of plants. "It's my vision that Ferrari-Carano gardens grow gracefully and continue to invoke a spirit of beauty for years to come."

Inspiration for home landscaping often comes from viewing unfamiliar plants or observing creative combinations in other people's gardens. Garden enthusiasts will be pleased with the thoughtful placement of identification markers for each plant grouping so they can adapt some of these ideas.

As pleasant as it is to stroll through the gardens, the culmination of the experience awaits visitors at Villa Fiore, where they can sip the Chardonnay, Fumé Blanc, Merlot, Zinfandel, Cabernet Sauvignon, and other fine wines that make Ferrari-Carano among the most respected wineries in the nation.

Ferrari-Carano Vineyards and Winery is located at 8761 Dry Creek Road, Healdsburg. For hours and information, call (707) 433-6700 or view the Web site at www.ferrari-carano.com.

Rancho Los Alamitos

Long Beach

Visiting Rancho Los Alamitos is like stepping back in time to the 1920s and 1930s—California's golden age of gardening. It's easy to imagine the lifestyle of that era because these gardens were created as practical outdoor living spaces, yet they also contain a wealth of visually appealing plant materials, many of which are still popular in modern gardens. The rancho was once the private residence of the Bixby family, but this artifact of Alta California is now a public historic site, where time has frozen the buildings and gardens into that of a long-lost era.

Like most California ranchos, this one originally covered a wide swath of land. Its 300,000 acres were a land grant deeded to Manuel Nieto in 1790. But by 1842, when it was acquired by Abel Stearns, it had shrunk to 28,500 acres with only a crude four-room adobe house used for vaqueros and ranch hands. In 1878, John Bixby, owner of Le Canon de Santa Ana Rancho, leased 1,000 acres of Rancho Los Alamitos along with the dilapidated adobe, and three years later with two partners, he acquired the entire Stearns place and moved his wife Susan and their son there. Susan Bixby, a keen gardening enthusiast, began the gardens while the adobe was enlarged to accommodate a growing family. By 1906, with both of his parents now dead, Fred Bixby and his children moved into the old ranch house, and it was due to efforts of his wife Florence that the gardens evolved over a thirty-year period to become a California showplace.

Seen here, a pair of century-old Moreton Bay fig trees, planted by Susan Bixby, are major design elements on the east lawn.

Florence's gardens exemplify restraint and simple beauty during an era when wealthy tycoons spent fortunes recreating grand European-styled gardens for their mansions. Florence hired talented landscape designers Florence Yoch and the Olmsted Brothers (successors to their famous father, Frederick Law Olmstead, who designed such notable spaces as New York's Central Park), who also designed the White House grounds and the Washington, D.C park system. For Florence Bixby, the Olmstead Brothers developed a series of garden rooms that encircle the ranch house and provide spaces for the indoor/outdoor living so popular in Southern California.

The gardens are intact today, although the passage of time has affected many of the plantings and hard-scape features, like the foundations and walkways. The non-profit Rancho Los Alamitos Foundation supervises ongoing garden restoration that began in 1993 as part of a comprehensive master plan project to restore the site with authentic historical accuracy and to interpret and reflect its place in California history. This process is a meticulous effort that, fortunately, is aided by the rancho's significant archive of Bixby family photographs, home movies, oral histories, drawings, plans, and written accounts.

Florence Bixby's gardens served as green buffers against the dry, dusty mesa surrounding the working ranch. She also took advantage of the view to ocean and to Catalina Island that the site afforded in her life-time. Today, though, modern housing developments

"Playdays," a bronze sculpture by Harriet Frismuth, is the focal point in the center of the decorative pool. It was a wedding anniversary gift to Florence Bixby from her husband.

Fragrant wisteria blooms in spring along the long Jacaranda Walk where the delicate green leaves of the century-old jacaranda trees provide shade.

block that view, and now the gardens serve as visual and aesthetic buffers to screen the gated community that surrounds the rancho.

Bixby and her designers created eleven distinct garden rooms surrounding the adobe house. Each has a different character and planting design, and patios and fountain areas are interspersed throughout, yet the gardens harmoniously flow into one another. The walled Secret Garden, with its garden art, statuary, and fountain was one of her favorite places for looking after her grandchildren or to go for quiet contemplation. She also added several long walks: the eighty-foot-long Geranium Walk, lined with geraniums in terra cotta pots; the eighty-foot-long Oleander Walk, planted with double-flowered oleanders and underplanted along the banks with blue plumbago capensis to screen out views of the housing developments; and the hundred-foot-long Jacaranda Walk adjacent to the tennis courts, where suitable young men could visit her teen-age daughters. Bixby also included themed gardens: a rose garden with a gazebo for enjoying the ocean view; a grape arbor; a "friendly" garden filled with cuttings given by friends; a rockery which later became a California native garden; the desert garden featuring cacti and succulents; and the Old Garden of softly colored flowering plants accented by a variety of green-leafed foliage plants.

Florence Bixby continued the tree planting that her mother-in-law had begun when she planted pepper trees

Following pages: The formal rose garden contains hybrid tea roses of the period, enclosed in boxwood hedges.

*Numerous pepper trees surround Rancho Los Alamitos
and create a privacy barrier from adjacent residences.
Here, clivia are in full bloom along the walkway.*

along the driveway and a pair of Moreton Bay fig trees
on the east lawn more than a century ago. Florence
admired palm trees and added many Canary Island and
Washingtonian palms, which, as they matured, became
guideposts for visitors to the ranch. She also planted
Torrey pine, rare for this region.

*Rancho Los Alamitos is located at 6400 Bixby Hill
Road, Long Beach, California, 90815. It is open to the
public Wednesday through Sunday afternoons from 1
to 5 p.m. For further information, call the Foundation
office, (562) 431-3541.*

Florence Bixby created the Friendly Garden, so named because
she continuously exchanged and received cuttings and seeds
from gardening friends.

Great swaths of daylilies border the walled patio where the Bixby family entertained guests.

Descanso Gardens

La Cañada

Visitors are in awe when they first go to Descanso Gardens. Shafts of sunlight stream through leafy canopies of gnarled, statuesque California live oak trees. Bird songs fill the air. In fall, winter, and early spring, magnificent, huge shrubs overflow with red, white, and multi-colored camellias.

All this beauty is adjacent to Los Angeles in 160-acres of forests, streams, California chaparral, and millions of flowers—a rarity in this region of congested freeways and burgeoning population. Here, in the largest camellia forest in North America , are 50,000 camellia shrubs, some soaring as high as thirty feet, growing in a twenty-five-acre oak forest.

Unlike most estate gardens, Descanso Gardens had mundane origins. Rather than a pleasure garden, it was founded as a commercial venture by E. Manchester Boddy, a prominent Los Angeles businessman, newspaper publisher, and visionary. When he first saw the site nestled along the San Rafael hills of La Cañada, some twenty miles north of downtown Los Angeles, he saw past the tangles of brambles, scrub and chaparral. He believed that camellia shrubs would thrive in the filtered light and rich soil in the hundred-year-old forest. In 1936 he took an option on the land, and planted twelve camellias to test his theory. They thrived; and he then purchased the entire 165-acre site in 1937 and started a commercial camellia nursery. Boddy named his venture Rancho del Descanso (Where I rest), and in 1938 built a

The Boddy House, built in 1938 as Boddy's residence, is now used as an art gallery and administrative offices.

Following pages: Seen here, the International Rosarium
contains thousands of roses and other plants. On the left
is Climbing Altissimo.

twenty-two-room mansion for the extravagant sum, at the time, of $140,000.

Boddy popularized camellias, especially for use in corsages, and he also encouraged their use as landscape plants throughout Southern California. At its peak, the grounds and greenhouses contained 600,000 camellia plants. His interests expanded to include lilacs and roses, and he hired a famed plantsman of the era, Walter Lammerts, who was regarded as the father of scientific rose breeding. While at Descanso, Dr. Lammerts created a rose history garden and such famous roses as Bewitched, Chrysler Imperial, Descanso Pillar, and Sunny June. He also influenced the world of flowering shrubs by creating lilacs for warm-winter areas. The Descanso series of lilacs includes the renowned Lavender Lady, which is still in great demand, and whose fragrance and color visitors can enjoy when they are in flower in their one-acre grove in March and April.

Camellias play a starring role, from mid-September when the pastel colors of sasanqua varieties unfurl their delicate petals. They're followed by the spectacular sight of many thousands of japonicas and reticulatas bursting into bloom a few months later. It's a rare treat to walk the dirt paths through the forest, savoring its earthy smells and marveling at the change of scenery and atmosphere.

Roses are also in abundance. The five-acre International Rosarium contains more than 3,700 antique and modern roses. This is an informal land-

Azaleas bloom in spring in the Japanese Garden.

scape, where the Queen of Flowers is showcased in landscape vignettes and planting beds among trees, flowering shrubs, and flowering perennials and annuals. Adjacent to a craftsman-style Rose Pavilion, streams, fountains, and a reflecting pond add the refreshing sounds of water.

Descanso Gardens is at its most beautiful in spring when tens of thousands of tulips, hyacinths, Dutch iris and other bulbs emerge in mid-March through April, and when flowering trees dazzle from above, creating a magnificent panoply of millions of blossoms.

Boddy sold Rancho del Descanso to the County of Los Angeles in 1953, and it was renamed Descanso Gardens when it was opened to the public, who now come from around the world to enjoy its beauty and

Above: The blue-roofed Tea House was built in 1966. Tea and light refreshments are served there on weekends.

Right: More than 50,000 camellia shrubs bloom fall through spring in the twenty-five-acre camellia forest.

wooded splendor. Visitors can also visit Boddy's former residence, The Boddy House, where monthly art shows and sales are held, and where local artists display paintings and sculptures in keeping with the floral setting.

Descanso Gardens is located at 1418 Descanso Drive, La Cañada, California 91011. It is open daily from 9 a.m. to 4: 30 p.m., except Christmas Day. For information, call (818) 952-4400.

*Bench bowers, custom made in England for
Descanso Gardens, invite visitors to linger in
the International Rosarium.*

*Flowering peach trees accent this meditative nook
adjacent to the Main Lawn and camellia forest.*

Stathatos Estate

San Marino

The small city of San Marino was once noted for its very large, secluded estates, like The Huntington, but over the last century, most of those grandiose places have been subdivided and houses built on their formerly undeveloped land. On one of them, where Jerry and Helen Stathatos's two-acre wooded estate is now located, Gabrielino Indians once trod the dirt path leading from the San Gabriel Mission to the Old Mill, a once-functioning grain mill in San Marino that supplied meal to the mission two centuries ago. The path, still clearly visible along the Stathatos' upper terrace, is flanked by centuries-old California live oak trees, a few of the many arboreal sentinels standing guard around their property. Other oaks, in a grove of more than a dozen gnarled trees, predate the 4,000-square-foot English country house that was built in 1939. In this very private enclave, the family is shielded from prying eyes by a perimeter planting of majestic sycamore, pecan, oak, and pittosporum trees, some more than 100 years old and soaring up to sixty feet. Dense myrtle hedges completely enclose the estate.

A local firm, Armstrong Nurseries, which is no longer in existence, initially designed the grounds of the estate, but when the Stathatoses bought it in 1963, they added a guesthouse, a swimming pool, an entertainment area, and expanded the gardens.

Jerry, an avid gardener whose business included the retail floral industry, fills his house with roses, daffodils,

Stately delphiniums and vibrant foxgloves greet visitors at the entrance to the Stathatos English country house.

Grand magnolia trees, at least a century old, shelter seating areas on the lawn's perimeter.

tulips, and other flowers from the gardens. He delights in weekend gardening and constantly experiments with new varieties of plants. He has his favorites: the gardens are filled with more than 100 roses, masses, of pastel or white azaleas, camellias, gardenias, and impatiens. It's an English cottage garden in harmony with the architecture of the house.

At the front entrance to the stone house, a majestic magnolia tree stands sentinel and a massive bird of paradise, the official flower of California, is in a place of honor near the entrance. Soft pink Bonica roses, deep blue lobelia, spicy pinks, and Shasta daisies border the flagstone entry walk. Elsewhere are more garden beds of Bonica roses, and masses of colorful bedding plants that are changed each season. Sensuous fragrance and color, and sweet night-blooming jasmine and blossoming citrus trees perfume the swimming pool and nearby guest house and patio.

These gardens are ideally suited for the fund-raising functions the Stathatoses hold for their favorite charities. At one memorable event for 300 alumnae of the University of California at Berkeley, the 150-member university band marched up the curving driveway and played for the astounded guests while they dined al fresco. Here, as at many other Southern California residences, large or small, the landscape is always a very important part of the outdoor life.

A massive Bird of Paradise, the official flower of Los Angeles, is given a place of honor near the entrance.

Clivia line a walk through the California live oak forest adjacent to the house.

Alden Estate

Santa Monica Canyon

Many estate gardens are noted for panoramic vistas of rolling lawns and adjacent landscapes. But in metropolitan regions like Los Angeles, privacy is valued as much as views. The Alden estate is a combination of dense plantings and intense privacy, provided by a large, one-acre wooded site with mature trees and shrubs that serve as efficient screens.

The one-acre estate is in Santa Monica Canyon, an area that has long been favored by artists, writers and Hollywood celebrities. The site was part of an old Spanish Land Grant, Rancho Boca de Santa Monica (Mouth of Santa Monica [Canyon]), containing natural springs, streams, sycamores and oaks, that was given to Francisca Marquez de Rios. After her death in 1902, the property was in legal limbo until the Santa Monica Land and Water Company purchased it in 1916. In 1928, Ella T. Fleming bought a two-acre parcel and hired architect Gordon P. Kaufman to build an eight-room stone and frame house in country French style.

Now owned by Hal and Geraldine Alden, the original estate has undergone several transformations by previous owners. Actress Loretta Young and baseball great Leo Durocher enlarged the house during the years they lived here in the 1940s. They sold it in 1952 and other famous owners included actor Frank Gorshin, who played Riddler in the TV series, *Batman*. In those years, a swimming pool and cabana was added and the driveway moved.

Although this estate is in the heart of metropolitan Los Angeles, the land-scape is characterized by dense, lush plantings. Here, Australian and New Zealand tree ferns provide cool shelter in this inviting seating area.

When the estate was offered for sale in 1971 it was subdivided, and what had been the gardener's cottage and guesthouse was given a separate address.

The Alden property now consists of the spacious house, pool with cabana, and a skillfully created series of garden rooms and pathways through the verdant landscape. A flagstone bridge constructed at the same time as the house leads from the terraces and flowerbeds across a stream into fern-filled shaded and secluded secret garden niches. The landscape includes centuries-old sycamore trees, 50-year-old camellia shrubs soaring to roof height, a massive redwood tree, azaleas, tree ferns, and carpets of ivies. When the Aldens acquired the property more than 20 years ago, they commissioned Helen Stulberg to enhance and beautify what was already planted. She did so by adding masses of flowering perennials, shrubs and trees in keeping with the naturalistic setting and informality of the architecture.

Like many designers, Stulberg believes in the design theory that a garden should yield its secrets as visitors stroll through it, with pathways beckoning to yet another sensory delight. And so it is in the Alden landscape, where stone or wood footpaths lead one through thickets of alders, past stately camellias, to seating nooks, secreted bird baths, or verdant hiding places.

Yet the entrance is a more traditional design, accented by stately ficus trees, Australian tree ferns and lush vibrant rhododendrons. Planting beds with daylilies, impatiens, campanula and agapanthus add hues of blue, yellow, pink and orange so the entrance is cheerful and inviting.

A formal rose garden, situated along the secluded west wing of the house, serves as a cutting garden and provides elegant blooms of the Bob Hope Rose, the Lagerfeld, Peace, Brandy, and other classic hybrid tea roses for enjoyment indoors.

Like many Southern California residences, outdoor spaces for relaxing and entertaining are important design components. Here, the landscape is like being in a country retreat, which is all the more remarkable in densely populated Los Angeles.

Following pages: Massive urns containing colorful annual plants punctuate the entrance. Plantings beds are filled with cascades of begonias, azaleas, calla lilies and rhododendrons.

Lotusland

Montecito

Southern California is young, in terms of gardening and architecture, compared to America's East Coast. Many of its homes and landscapes sprang into existence after World War II, but there are some historic estates where the landscape was designed more than a century ago and plants installed that still flourish. In these great gardens trees have attained their mature growth, foundation plants have established their patterns and rhythms, and often, unusual plants can be seen. Such a garden is Lotusland, whose influence extends far beyond its 37 acres, and where garden lovers can marvel at fascinating landscape design and rare plants in unusual combinations. It's unlike any other garden in America, perhaps even the world, because of the flamboyantly bold forms and unusual color combinations and types of plants in the collections.

The gardens were created in 1882 by pioneer nurseryman R. Kenton Stevens, who planted palms, exotic trees, and other subtropical plants on the site when he started his nursery. At the time, the site was named Tanglewood because of its many oak trees and shrubby undergrowth. Many of the original plantings remain, including more than 100 varieties of palm trees; many of which are now endangered in their native habitats.

The gardens have undergone several major transformations during their evolution. In the early 1900s, Mr. and Mrs. E. Palmer Gavit bought the land and hired local expert Peter Riedel to transform the nursery into actual

Blue fescue grass covers the winding path through the Blue Garden. It's bordered by large pieces of slag glass, formerly used in the manufacture of Coca-Cola bottles.

Abalone shells form the perimeter of a pond and are decorative accents in the Aloe Garden.

gardens. A pink Spanish tile and stucco house, designed in 1919 by Reginald Johnson, was later remodeled by the celebrated Santa Barbara architect George Washington Smith, who added a swimming pool, bathhouse, and a pink perimeter wall that remains as a landmark. The Spanish-style estate was named Cuesta Linda.

In 1941, the flamboyant Polish opera singer Madame Ganna Walska, who had married and outlived six very rich husbands, bought the estate and spent forty years, until her death in 1984, supervising every aspect of its transformation. She renamed it Lotusland, although she wasn't the first to grow these water plants (Stevens was one of the first Americans to grow the plant that is sacred to India). Madame Walska regarded Lotusland as her spiritual retreat from the world, and eventually she established the Ganna Walska Lotusland Foundation to maintain her beloved creation and to have it opened occasionally for public visits.

As Madame Walska modified the gardens, she consulted two of the region's most famous landscape architects, Lockwood de Forest and Ralph T. Stevens (son of Kinton Stevens). She also consulted expert horticulturists when she wanted to showcase her increasing botanical collections of aloes, bromeliads, cycads, cacti and succulents. Lotusland is famous for its renowned collection of cycads, ancient plants that are a cross between a palm and a conifer, some species of which are now extinct in the wild.

The aloe garden displays a collection of more than 100 different kinds of aloes.

Lotusland is also renowned for its sculptural plants, like the dramatic cacti and euphorbia that grow up to the rooftop in front of the main house. Many are also displayed in the twenty-two distinct garden "rooms." The Blue Garden contains only trees and plants with hues of blue/green foliage, including a grove of blue Atlas cedars, blue spruce, and Mexican blue palms. Blue fescue grass covers the ground, and the winding path is lined with pieces of slag glass that was once used in making Coca-Cola bottles. Abalone shells border an abalone pond; the shells are placed in groupings to create the image of a lotus unfurled. It leads to the aloe garden containing hundreds of different kinds of aloes on display in massive groupings. Madame Walska also added an outdoor theater where various musical performances were staged among the tightly manicured hedges. There, vying for attention, are grotesque dwarf

Madame Walska experimented freely with bold forms and unusual combinations. Here Spanish moss cascades down to spiny cacti and succulent plants.

Formally clipped hedges, mosaics, and a fountain decorate a parterre behind the main house.

figures of men and women in eighteenth-century garb transported from her French chateau.

Although Madame Walska spent considerable time and effort to create these complex and daring gardens, she also had several traditional, formal landscapes designed. A parterre adjacent to a conventional fruit tree orchard near the rear of the main house leads to a topiary garden, in which she had created a massive floral clock that actually tells the time. And there is only one green meadow on the property—a great swath of lawn near the house.

Devotees of more traditional gardens will enjoy strolling the meandering shore of the lake that is the heart of the five-acre Japanese garden. It has flowering cherry trees, bonsai shrubs, and an impressive collection of Japanese lanterns, statues, and other garden adornments, and each turn of the path leads to yet another visual delight, such as the authentic Shinto shrine nestled among the Japanese cedar trees.

Guided walking tours of Ganna Walska Lotusland occur mid-February through mid-November, Wednesday through Saturday. Tours are available by reservation only, and are usually filled well in advance because of parking restrictions. To schedule a tour, phone (805) 969-9990.

Virginia Robinson Estate & Gardens

Beverly Hills

Henry and Virginia Robinson created their dream house and beautiful gardens in Beverly Hills when this community was in its infancy. Fortunately for admirers of exquisite gardens and history, Virginia Robinson willed her house and property at her death in 1977 to the County of Los Angeles for public viewing. "The Robinson Gardens is more in the class of a museum," director Tim Lindsay explained. "It's like stepping back in time to a more serene, peaceful era." Because of restrictions placed by local residents, who don't want hordes of people invading their residential area, viewing is by reservation only on Tuesdays through Fridays, by docent-led tours. This is the only house of its kind in Beverly Hills open for public viewing.

Harry and Virginia were married in 1903. When they returned from their three-year honeymoon in Europe and India, they bought fifteen acres of land from the founder of Beverly Hills, Burton Green. On this land, Virginia's father, architect Nathaniel Dryden, built for the Robinsons a handsome Mediterranean Classic Revival house. Completed in 1911, the house was furnished with artifacts the Robinsons collected while on their honeymoon. It is now listed on the National Register of Historic Places.

The 6,000-square-foot house contains just six main rooms: parlor-sitting room; dining room; morning room; library; bedroom; and kitchen with utility area. The rooms are furnished as they were when Mrs. Robinson

Following pages: Masses of bearded iris provide vertical exclamation points of color near the entrance to the Virginia Robinson Estate and Gardens.

The Renaissance Revival Pool Pavilion, built in 1924, is modeled after the famous Villa Pisani in Italy.

died in 1977, and a grandfather clock in the entrance is stopped at 6:20, the time of her death.

The estate grounds, now encompassing 6.5 acres, are divided into five areas, each with a distinct theme. French doors open from the house to the central Mall, with the character of an English walled garden, with herbaceous borders, sweeping manicured lawns flanked with stately Italian cypress trees, statuary, and a vista; Mrs. Robinson used this lovely space as an outdoor entertaining area. Pathways lead to a lawn-flanked swimming pool containing mosaic tile wainscoting. The adjacent pool pavilion was built in 1924 by architect William Richards. This building blends Palladian and eighteenth-century Italian architectural influences and was modeled after the famous Villa Pisani in Italy.

The Italian and Mediterranean influence continues west of the Mall in the Italian Terrace garden, with its brick paths, terraces, fountains, ponds, statuary, urns, and a Mediterranean plant palette including groves of citrus trees. This part of the landscape is also filled with majestic trees, including fir and magnolias, and offers sweeping views over the surrounding region.

Virginia Robinson loved plants and had an eclectic assortment. She filled the shady northern parts of her gardens with camellias, azaleas, and brilliant hues of clivia.

She was also intrigued by tropical plants, and created a tropical palm garden containing the largest collection of Australian King palms in the continental United

The Terrace Garden offers views of terraced citrus. It's
bordered by a variety of camellias.

A pair of lions, imported from Italy, guard the Italian Terrace Garden.

States. Within this moist, cool, verdant glade are also gingers, bananas, plumeria, and many other exotic specimens with dramatic textures, foliage, and flowers.

Mrs. Robinson also enjoyed roses and created a rose garden. Currently undergoing restoration, this garden contains 800 antique and modern bushes. Roses are also planted elsewhere on the property, including at the entrance where dazzling white Iceberg Roses are accented by stately iris and bay laurel hedges.

The estate also contains an area for growing herbs and vegetables. Its kitchen garden is planted in an area resembling a French potager, with easy access for harvesting fresh herbs and seasonal produce.

The Robinson Estate and Gardens is the quintessential Southern California landscape with an eclectic mix of plants that thrive in this hospitable climate.

For touring information or reservations, call 310-276-5367.

Following pages: Graceful Italian cypress trees punctuate a long border filled with a kaleidoscope of brilliantly colored flowers.

Beaulieu

Napa Valley

Majestic London plane trees stand as silent sentinels, ushering fortunate guests down a long driveway onto the grounds of Beaulieu. Founded almost 100 years ago by Monsieur and Madame George de Latour, Beaulieu boasts vast swaths of verdant lawns, bordered by ancient trees, laurel hedges, paths, and shaded walkways. Now owned by the Sullivan family, descendents of the de Latours, and no longer encompassing the winery for which it was once well known, Beaulieu remains one of the oldest and finest estates in Napa Valley, where excellence in gardens is pursued as relentlessly as excellence in fine wines.

The tree-lined driveway bisects the vineyards and leads to the main residence, first constructed in 1910 as the manager's house. The house is primarily of Queen Anne design, as interpreted by Sernande de Latour. The white, wooden, one-story house has evolved into an elegant and quintessential California residence. Bordering the house are walkways planted with English laurel hedges, underplanted with seasonal annuals. Encompassing the house is a nine-acre landscape initially created by the de Latours almost 100 years ago.

This grand landscape is quietly formal—a California adaptation of French and Italian design styles—with clean lines and crisp angles. Wide gravel pathways connect the various segments within the gardens. At one point, visitors can admire the famous sunken Italian Garden, which contains a rectangular pond filled with

Sculpted dark green cypress and tree roses border a secret fountain.

water lilies and resplendent goldfish. Another pathway leads to a hidden fountain, bordered by dark sculpted cypress. Further, beautiful Italian statues ornament the gardens and serve as focal points, when prominently displayed, or as secret riches to be discovered, in the many secluded nooks.

Throughout the grounds, flowers are used as accents in defined plantings. One example is a formal rose garden with neatly arranged beds—containing some classic hybrid tea roses, such as sweetly perfumed Double Delight, legendary Peace, stately Queen Elizabeth, and vibrant Tropicana—bordered by manicured boxwood hedges. Other accents include at one point jasmine and bedding begonias, at another point white agapanthus and containers full of white petunias. Great trees, including a 400-year-old oak, evoke a sense of timelessness.

One of the most famous features at Beaulieu is an L-shaped walkway bordered with plane trees in a form known as "pleached," a horticultural technique where branches are trained to intertwine. It took more than 30 years of skilled pruning and trellising to shape Beaulieu's

Seen here, the Italian sunken garden is the signature feature at this estate.

plane trees into their present form. This walkway and the sunken Italian Garden are the signature garden features of Beaulieu.

These gardens are stately and majestic. They also have had practical purposes, being on occasion made to serve as settings for garden parties, for diverse social and charitable occasions.

Dagmar Sullivan, granddaughter of the founders, is the current owner of Beaulieu, along with her four children. Although the family doesn't now live there full-time, the property continues to suggest the interests of an active family. There is a tennis court, with climbing roses around the perimeter fencing. And a fruit orchard and vegetable garden that once supplied the kitchen still yields abundant harvests of French plums, artichokes, and, of course, table grapes.

In pleasant contrast to the formality of the gardens, an atmosphere of charming informality is in places suggested—thanks to the Napa River creek flowing through the grounds. Sloping banks are covered with four-o'clocks, which unfurl their bright blue flowers on languid spring afternoons. The line of blue-flowering agapanthus along the creek echoes their hue.

Pages 150–151: Ancient oaks line a driveway leading to the estate. The Napa Creek trickles below the sloping bank.

Hacienda Mar Monte

Pebble Beach

In 1929, prominent Monterey Bay architect Robert Stanton bought a prime, 2.9-acre hillside site, in what is now Pebble Beach, near the peninsula's famous 17-Mile-Drive. He built an imposing 9,000-square-foot, seven bedroom house in evocative Spanish style that capitalized on the spectacular views of Carmel Beach, Point Lobos, and the Pacific Ocean, and fittingly named the estate Hacienda Mar Monte.

Present owners Finis and Julie Conner adapted the original design to reflect their love of Italy and Spain, and redecorated the house in the Mediterranean style. At the time of their purchase, much of the hilly and steep grounds hadn't been planted, but since then the landscape has been totally transformed, although many of the ancient oak and cypress trees were left untouched.

With the assistance of landscape designer Richard Murray, the Conners created three broad lawn terraces on the steep site. They ascend gracefully from the driveway entrance to the house, and made it possible to install a heated outdoor swimming pool and spa, a croquet lawn, a putting green for Finis (who is an accomplished golfer), and a level section for entertaining.

Julie, an enthusiastic gardener who loves roses and brightly colored flowers, planted beds of brightly blooming annuals and perennials that mark the driveway entrance and accent the entrance to the house. Antique stone topiaries flank steps that end in paths winding through the flower gardens, where one can enjoy the

Foxgloves and agapanthus bloom in the foreground of one of three broad lawn terraces overlooking Carmel Beach and Point Lobos.

Oaks, cypress, and citrus trees surround the formal landscape. The pool is heated for continuous use throughout the year.

sights, sounds, and aromas in secret seating areas. One such nook contains a fountain accented by trailing lavender flowers, and a carefully placed stone bench where one can sit and view the lovely formal rose garden's 80 hybrid tea and floribunda roses.

In designing the landscape, the Conners were careful to preserve the extraordinary views that make this estate one of the finest in the region. Around aged trees, like the statuesque Norfolk Island pine planted in the early twentieth century, they carefully placed accent trees that augmented those stands without blocking the views. Near the swimming pool and spa a graceful weeping cedar is in an area where trees and shrubbery create a study in greens and browns. Hues of silver and purple are brought into the picture by graceful wisteria vines and lavender shrubs that add sweet fragrance in spring and summer. Large boulders near the water serve as "diving boards."

Ancient oaks near the house hide a secret garden defined by manicured boxwood hedges, and entered through ornamental iron gates. Within, gentle sounds of water can be heard from a tile fountain, and also from a natural spring that flows nearby, as well as from fountains and birdbaths elsewhere in the garden. A small herb garden filled with aromatic basils, thyme, rosemary and other kitchen herbs surrounds an antique bird bath, and in other places the gardens attract hummingbirds who come to sip nectar from penstemon plants,

Massive oaks shelter a secret garden containing a tiled fountain and formal rose garden.

bougainvillea, and other nectar-laden flowers. Bees and butterflies hover over the roses, lavender and herbs.

The Conners have brought elements of Mediterranean landscape to their gardens by including lemon and cypress trees as well as brightly colored bougainvillea that entwines through the balustrade of the upper balcony and also decorates the courtyard walls. More climbing flowers capture the eye when Cl. Cecile Brunner bursts forth in thousands of clear pink flowers every spring and summer. Horse chestnut trees add their pink floral tones in spring, too.

The gardens were planned to provide ample room for entertainment and other activities, including events for numerous charitable, social and civic organizations, and fund-raising events during the year. And the Conners also open their gardens for benefit tours each spring and fall.

The Huntington Library,
Art Collections &
Botanical Gardens

San Marino

The influence that Henry Huntington exerted on the California of a century ago was great, and the effects continue to be felt to this day. In particular, we can look to his estate and gardens, which set a standard for excellence then, and continue to exist now as a model of exquisite taste.

Huntington made his fortune in the railroad industry during the late nineteenth and early twentieth century. Subsequently, he purchased vast tracts of land in Southern California and helped develop the region that he believed would become one of America's leading commercial centers.

Among his purchases in 1903 was a 600-acre citrus, fruit, avocado, and nut ranch in San Marino. Admiring its setting in the San Gabriel Valley, Huntington decided it would serve well as the location for his permanent residence. With this end in mind, he hired prominent Los Angeles architects Myron Hunt and Elmer Grey to build his Beaux-Arts mansion. The mansion took several years to construct, and Huntington and his wife Arabella did not move into it until 1914. They dwelled there together until the death of Arabella in 1924; Henry passed on in 1927. A mausoleum on the site contains their remains. Before their deaths, Henry and Arabella created a non-profit trust and established a research institution to serve scholars. The institution opened to the public as The Huntington Library, Art Collections and Botanical Gardens in 1928.

The Italian baroque fountain is the focal point of the North Vista, also ornamented with seventeenth-century stone statues portraying allegorical and mythological subjects.

While his wife collected art and decorative furnishings, Henry collected rare books and manuscripts—and he collected rare plants. Huntington delighted in finding unusual trees and plants, and he brought them to his estate from around the world. Before his house was completed, Huntington's plant collections had grown to a considerable size; seeking to transform the ranch into an estate garden to house this collection, he hired landscape designer William Hertrich, who helped bring Huntington's vision to fruition.

The Huntington is an estate laid out in classic design, with great swaths of green lawns, expansive vistas, allées, beautiful statuary, fountains, ponds, and a wide variety of gardens dedicated to distinctive plant groups or landscape design. One of the great benefits of visiting The Huntington is the opportunity to observe mature plants—some of which have come from distant regions and lands—that have withstood both the test of time and as well the region's climatic conditions. The estate now consists of 207 acres, of which 150 are landscaped and open to public viewing.

Historically, the gardens began at the Lily Pond, waterfall, and adjacent jungle garden. The ponds contain lilies, lotuses, turtles, koi, and migrant mallards. Huntington's famous bamboo collection, consisting of more than fifty different kinds, is nearby. A massive clump of giant timber bamboo, on the east side of the ponds, was planted in 1906. Entering the jungle garden,

visitors can view gingers, ferns, orchids, philodendrons, and bromeliads growing beneath the forest canopy. Encircling two sides of the jungle garden is the palm garden, containing more than 200 species of the best palms for Southern California's cold, wet winters and hot, dry summers. Palms were among Huntington's favorite trees and when the five-acre garden was first planted in 1905 mature palm trees were transplanted from other parts of Southern California to give it an aged appearance. He also imported palms from around the world to evaluate their suitability to the climate. As a result, many parks, streets, and highways in Southern California are graced with Chilean wine palms, Canary Island date palms, and Mediterranean fan palms.

One of the most famous and distinguished gardens at The Huntington is the desert garden. Within these

Several large beds of David Austin English Roses bloom in the Rose Garden. First planted in 1908, the Rose Garden features thousands of different modern and Old Garden Roses growing in beds, on pergolas, and over arbors and arches.

The Herb Garden contains demonstration beds filled with herbs historically used for culinary, medicinal, and cosmetic purposes.

twelve acres are more than 10,000 species of succulents and desert plants from arid regions around the world. This is one of the world's largest outdoor collections of cacti and succulents.

The rose garden, which was established in 1908 as a strolling garden for Arabella and her guests, is also an outstanding display. Visitors can walk beneath rose-laden pergolas and admire the approximately 4,000 roses, consisting of 1,500 cultivars, that make up the collection. This is a formal rose garden, so termed because it's arranged in beds. There are forty at the Huntington, organized by years in which specific varieties were grown or hybridized. Old Garden Roses, those grown before 1867, occupy one long bed along the north pergola. Benches are placed strategically throughout the garden, clustered under magnificent magnolia trees and along the sweeping St. Augustine lawn. Visitors are encouraged to walk along the lawn and view the beds of English and French shrub roses planted in the garden's interior. Henry and Arabella strolled along a central walkway, beneath stately arches now covered with a collection of climbing roses, including the antique Belle of Portugal and the new, multi-hued Polka. Continue in their footsteps to a massive twenty-foot dome, covered with myriad blossoms of Mermaid.

In addition to being a research garden, this rose garden evokes romance. A winding pathway leads to an eighteenth-century French stone tempietto containing a statue entitled, "Love, the Captive of Youth," depicting Cupid and his captor, a fair maiden. A bed of French Lace Roses encircles the setting.

An equally popular spot is the Japanese Garden, said to have been a wedding gift to Arabella to entice her to move to California. The nine-acre garden is one of the most mature gardens of its kind in America. In addition to the tranquil garden, with lily ponds and streams, visitors can view an authentic Japanese house, experience a dry Zen garden, and view thirty meticulously trained bonsai.

In late fall and winter camellias are in full bloom. The Huntington's camellia collection is comprehensive and artistically displayed in both the Japanese garden and along the North Vista, a grand allée bordered by seventeenth-century limestone statues. The sweeping lawn once served as the family's croquet court.

The herb and Shakespeare gardens are also noteworthy. The herb garden was once Arabella's cutting garden. Now it contains informative displays of herbs traditionally used for cooking, medicines, and cosmetics. The Shakespeare Garden showcases plants mentioned in the Bard's writings.

A visit to The Huntington isn't complete without a tour of the mansion, which contains priceless works of art, including the famous "Blue Boy," by Gainsborough, and "Pinkie," by Sir Thomas Lawrence. The spacious rooms are also filled with statuary and decorative art.

The Huntington is located at 1151 Oxford Road, San Marino, California 91108. It is open Tuesday through Friday: noon to 4:30 p.m.; Saturday and Sunday: 10:30 a.m. to 4:30 p.m. For information, call (818) 405-2141.

Wisteria frames the moon bridge in the Japanese Garden, distinguished by curving walks, flowing water, still lakes, painstakingly-pruned trees and shrubs, and artistically placed stones.

Please
Stay On
Concrete
Walk

Index